Managing Editor
Ina Massler Levin, M.A

Editor-in-Chief
Sharon Coan, M.S. Ed.

Illustrator
Ken Tunell

Cover Artist
Brenda DiAntonis

Art Coordinator
Kevin Barnes

Imaging
Alfred Lau
Temo Parra

Product Manager
Phil Garcia

Publishers
Rachelle Cracchiolo, M.S. Ed.
Mary Dupuy Smith, M.S. Ed.

Patriotic Monuments & Memorials

Author

Melissa Hart, M.F.A.

Teacher Created Materials, Inc.
6421 Industry Way
Westminster, CA 92683
www.teachercreated.com
ISBN-0-7439-3598-5
©2002 Teacher Created Materials, Inc.
Made in U.S.A.

Table of Contents

Introduction to Teachers

Patriotic Monuments & Memorials provides students with the history of some of the most famous landmarks in the United States, as well as some which are not so well known. It moves from the numerous monuments in Washington, D.C., to memorials which commemorate the work of great Americans including Jane Addams, Harriet Tubman, and Martin Luther King, Jr.

Students will learn about Mount Rushmore and its lesser-known neighbor, the Crazy Horse Memorial. They will explore museums, including the Smithsonian Institution and the United States Holocaust Memorial Museum. Working political monuments—such as the Supreme Court and the United Nations—will also be discussed. Near the end of the book, students will learn about national parks and preserves. They will have the opportunity to research and report on these, as well.

Patriotic Monuments & Memorials not only provides students with history but also with the opportunities to create their own monuments, research other memorials, answer riddles, and prepare recipes inspired by different Americans.

The Capitol Building

The United States Congress meets in the Capitol Building, located in Washington, D.C. When George Washington (1732–1799) was president, members of Congress met in several different cities. In 1790, they decided to choose a permanent location for the capital. The states of Maryland and Virginia gave land for what is known as the District of Columbia, or Washington D.C. Washington, D.C. was named after our first president. It is not part of any state.

A physician named William Thornton designed the Capitol Building. On September 18, 1793, George Washington laid the cornerstone of the Capitol Building. The Capitol is mostly built of white marble. The dome is made of iron. A sculpture of a woman decorates the top of the dome. She represents freedom.

During the War of 1812, British soldiers burned the Capitol building. It was rebuilt after the war. Since its construction in the 1700s, the Capitol Building has been expanded to more than twice its original size. Important parts of the building include the Rotunda (directly under the dome), the Senate Chamber in the north wing, the House Chamber in the south wing, the President's Room, and the National Statuary Hall. This hall contains statues of important

Answer these questions to have fast facts about the Capitol.

1. Our Capitol Building was built in _____.

2. Our nation's capital is not located in any state. It is in an area called _____

_____

3. The Capitol Building is mostly built of _____

4. Since its construction in the 1700s, the Capitol Building has been expanded to _____

_____.

5. Three of the most important parts of the Capitol Building are _____

_____, _____.

Picture Puzzle

Cut out the puzzle pieces. Glue them together on a piece of construction paper. Write the name of the important landmark in Washington, D.C. at the top of construction paper. Write five facts about this building below the picture.

The Washington Monument

The Washington Monument is located at the end of the National Mall, near the Capitol Building in Washington, D.C. It was built to honor George Washington, who was the first president of the United States from 1789 to 1797. It took nearly a century for the idea of this monument to become a reality. The United States government was slow in finding money for the monument, so a group of private citizens in the 1830s raised the money to bring their dream to life.

The cornerstone of the monument was laid in 1848 with the same shovel Washington had used in 1793 to lay the cornerstone of the Capitol Building. Construction on the Washington Monument took a long time. Political tensions, lack of money, and the Civil War were responsible for several holds on the building process. The monument was finally completed in 1884.

The Washington Monument is made of stone. A pyramid made of aluminum sits on top of it. The monument was modeled after a classic Egyptian obelisk. At 555 feet (169 m) tall it is one of the tallest masonry structures in the world. The inner walls of the monument are made of marble. There are 896 steps leading to an observation room at the top. Here, visitors can look out windows and see the Lincoln Memorial, the Capitol Building, the White House, and the Jefferson Memorial.

Activity: Create a model of the Washington Monument by following directions on page 7.

Make a Washington Monument

Follow these directions to make a model of the Washington Monument.

- Cut on the dark black lines.
- Fold on the dotted lines.
- Fold the top points in towards the center.
- Tuck the tabs, and tape or glue together the sides
- Tape the top together.

Stand the monument on a piece of drawing paper and add a reflecting pool.

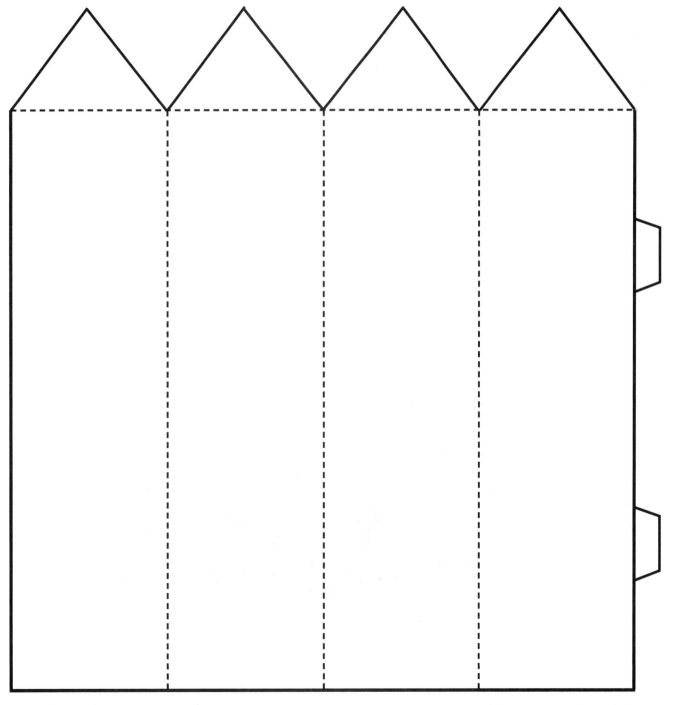

The White House

The White House was the first public building to be built in Washington, D.C. Construction began in 1792 and was completed in 1800. It has been the home of every American president with the exception of George Washington.

The White House is made of Virginia sandstone. It sits on 18.07 acres (7.31 hectares). The first floor is made up of formal rooms of state, where receptions are held. This floor is open to the public. On the second floor, you'll find the President's private rooms. Rooms for guests and staff are located on the third floor.

During the War of 1812, British troops set the White House on fire, destroying its interior. Repairs took five years. Between 1948 and 1952, President Harry S. Truman asked for the walls of the White House to be strengthened by new foundations and steel bars.

Throughout its history, the White House has had several names. It has been called the President's Palace, the President's House, and the Executive Building. Theodore Roosevelt had the name "The White House" put on his stationery in 1901. From then on, this is what people have called the president's house.

Activity: Visit the Web site for the White House at *www.whitehouse.gov*. Explore the site. Write a short summary of your favorite part of the site.

White House Pets

Presidents and their families have had many pets live with them in the White House. President John F. Kennedy's daughter had a pet named Macaroni. Can students guess what kind of pet Macaroni was? Students can find out all about kids and their pets that have lived in the White House by completing the following activity.

Before the computer:

Ask students the question, Who lives in the White House? Discuss the pets that have lived there and what it might be like for them to live in the White House. Ask students if they have ever visited the White House. Using the Internet link below, take the class on a virtual tour of the White House led by Spotty, George W. Bush's English springer spaniel. Explain that other presidents have also had pets. Brainstorm a list of pets that could live in the White House.

On the computer:

Have students work with partners to explore the White House for Kids home page. They can discover the type of pets that live at the White House.

After the computer:

Have the students share their recorded data and tell interesting facts about pets in the White House.

Internet Link:

The White House for Kids
http://www.whitehouse.gov/kids/html/index.html

Activities:

1. Draw a White House pet and write one interesting fact about it. Older students may write a report.

2. Take a class pet survey and create a bar graph to show the type and number of pets owned by students.

3. Make a class book titled "Our Pets." Let each student contribute a page. For students who do not have pets, let them write about a pet they would like to have.

4. Write the directions for the care and feeding of a family pet.

The Jefferson Memorial

The Jefferson Memorial in Washington, D.C., was built to honor Thomas Jefferson (1743–1826). Jefferson served as the third president of the United States, from 1801 to 1809. He also wrote the Declaration of Independence.

The Jefferson Memorial was built of white marble. It is circular, with 26 columns around it. The ceiling is dome-shaped. Construction on the Jefferson Memorial began in 1939. The building was dedicated in 1943. This monument is surrounded by hundreds of Japanese cherry trees.

Visitors who walk into the Jefferson Memorial will see a bronze statue of Thomas Jefferson, who stands facing the White House. Parts of the Declaration of Independence are inscribed on white marble inside the memorial. Visitors can learn what Thomas Jefferson thought about freedom, independence, and democracy.

Activity: Thomas Jefferson wrote in the Declaration of Independence, "We hold these truths to be self-evident, that all men are created equal, that they are endowed by their Creator with certain unalienable rights, that among these are life, liberty, and the pursuit of happiness." In your own words, explain what he meant by this sentence. Use the lines below.

The Lincoln Memorial

Abraham Lincoln (1809–1865) served as the sixteenth president of the United States, from 1861 to 1865. His dedication to America during the Civil War earned him the reputation of being kind and fair, as well as very strong. Abraham Lincoln grew up poor in the backwoods of Kentucky and Indiana. Through hard work and studying, he earned a place in politics, eventually becoming a beloved leader.

The Lincoln Memorial was built from marble, granite, and limestone in 1914. The Memorial was dedicated on February 12, 1922, on Lincoln's birthday. Outside the Lincoln Memorial, visitors will find 36 columns, which represent the states in the Union at the time of Lincoln's death in 1865. There are three chambers inside the memorial. The first features a marble statue of Abraham Lincoln. Visitors to the south chamber can read Lincoln's Gettysburg Address inscribed in white marble. The north chamber houses an inscription of Lincoln's Second Inaugural Address.

The Memorial has been the site of many famous events since its construction. Famed African-American singer Marian Anderson sang there in 1939. In 1963, Martin Luther King, Jr., delivered his famous "I Have a Dream" speech at the Lincoln Memorial.

Activity: Visit the following Web site: *www.whitehouse.gov.* Find and read the biography of Abraham Lincoln. Then on a separate sheet of paper list three interesting facts that you discovered about his life.

Photo Opportunity!

The *Microsoft Encarta Encyclopedia* allows you to view a photograph of the Lincoln Memorial from a 360-degree angle.

Arlington National Cemetery

The Arlington National Cemetery is a federal burial ground located in Virginia. It stretches more than 612 acres (248 hectares) and contains the bodies of over 240,000 veterans and their dependent children, as well as political leaders. Most people buried in the Arlington National Cemetery fought with the United States armed forces and were killed in battle. Famous Americans buried here include Presidents John F. Kennedy and William H. Taft, political leader Robert F. Kennedy, author William Jennings Bryan, and explorers Admiral Robert E. Peary and Matthew Henson.

In 1863, during the Civil War, the land that the Arlington National Cemetery occupies now was taken from Confederate general Robert E. Lee's wife, Mary Anna. Arlington House, the former mansion in which Mary Anna and her husband lived in, still stands on the grounds of the Arlington Cemetery.

In 1863, part of the land became Freedman's Village—a settlement for former slaves. Freedman's Village lasted thirty years.

The Arlington National Cemetery is also home to the Tomb of the Unknown Soldier. The Tomb stands as a memorial to all unidentified soldiers who were killed in combat. In 1921, an unidentified soldier who had died in France was buried in the Arlington National Cemetery. A marble tomb was placed on his grave in 1932. Several unidentified soldiers from later wars were also buried here.

Activity: Visit the following Web site and look at the photos of Arlington National Cemetery. Go to *www.arlingtoncemetery.org* and click on Photo Gallery. On a separate page, describe one of the photos and how it made you feel as you looked at it.

The Smithsonian Institution

The Smithsonian Institution has its headquarters in Washington, D.C. The British scientist James Smithson inspired the creation of the Institute in 1846. It sponsors scientific research and exploration, publishes books, and maintains the national collections of the United States. The library of the Smithsonian Institution contains over 1.2 million books.

The Smithsonian Institution is made up of 14 museums and galleries, as well as the National Zoo in Washington, D.C. The National Museum of the American Indian and Cooper-Hewitt National Design Museum in New York City are also part of the Institution.

Activity: Find out more about this fascinating institution by visiting their Web site at *www.si.edu*. Choose two of the museums to research and answer the questions below.

1. What is the name of this museum or gallery?

_____

_____

2. What would you see if you went there?

_____

_____

_____

_____

_____

1. What is the name of this museum or gallery?

_____

_____

2. What would you see if you went there?

_____

_____

_____

_____

_____

Marine Corps Memorial

The Marine Corps War Memorial was built to honor those soldiers in the United States Marine Corps who died in battle. In 1945, sculptor Felix W. de Weldon saw a photograph that Joe Rosenthal had taken. The photo showed soldiers raising an American flag on Iwo Jima, an island near Japan. De Weldon was so inspired by the picture that he designed a life-sized sculpture. Three of the six soldiers from Rosenthal's photograph posed for the sculpture. De Weldon used pictures of the other three soldiers, who had died in battle, to complete the faces on his sculpture.

The sculpture's plaster cast was sent to New York to be cast in bronze. This process took three years. The bronze soldiers stand 32 feet high. They are shown erecting a flagpole, from which a cloth flag flies 24 hours a day. An inscription on the base of the memorial reads: "In honor and in memory of the men of the United States Marine Corps who have given their lives to their country since November 10, 1775."

The Marine Corps War Memorial is located in Washington, D.C.

Activity: Pretend you are one of the men who raised the American flag at Iwo Jima during World War II. Write a journal entry below describing how you might feel about the United States and fighting in the war.

_____

_____

_____

_____

_____

_____

_____

_____

_____

_____

_____

**United States Marine Corps
War Memorial**

Vietnam Veterans Memorial

The Vietnam Veterans Memorial is located in Washington, D.C. It was built to honor those soldiers who died or were declared missing during the Vietnam War (1959–1975).

The memorial was designed by a 21-year old student of architecture, Maya Ying Lin. It was built in 1982. The memorial is over 493 feet (150 m) long. It is shaped like a V, and it is made of black granite. The walls are inscribed with over 58,000 names of soldiers.

In 1984, Frederick Hart added his sculpture, The Three Servicemen, to the Vietnam Veterans Memorial. In 1993, Glenda Goodacre contributed her bronze sculpture, titled The Vietnam Women's Memorial. This last sculpture shows three nurses and a wounded soldier. It honors the over 11,000 American women who served in the Vietnam War.

Activity: Go to the Web site *http://www.VirtualWall.org/iStates.htm.* Choose a state and a soldier. Then answer the questions below.

1. What is the name of the person you chose?

   _____

   _____

2. Where did this person live?

   _____

   _____

3. What job did he/she hold in the United States Armed Forces?

   _____

   _____

4. On what panel and line number from the Vietnam Veterans Memorial would you find this person?

   _____

   _____

5. What interesting details did you find out about this person from what other people wrote about him/her?

   _____

   _____

Washington, D.C.

Have students apply mapping skills to place a monument located in Washington, D.C., on a classroom map of the Mall area. They research their monument and provide a drawing and information to accompany the map. Students can research using the Internet and key words. They may also use research books and encyclopedias.

Materials Needed:

- enlarge map of the Mall and surrounding area on poster board (See page 19.)
- name of seven monuments written on, or affixed to, note cards (See below.)
- seven copies of page 18, one for each group
- seven 3" x 5" note cards
- seven additional note cards
- construction paper

1. The Vietnam Veterans Memorial
2. Arlington National Cemetery
3. The Jefferson Memorial
4. The Lincoln Memorial
5. The Marine Corps War Memorial
6. The Roosevelt Memorial
7. The Washington Monument

Washington, D.C. *(cont.)*

Enlarge the map of the Mall on page 19 (label only the Capitol Building and Smithsonian Castle) onto a sheet of poster board. Display it along with the names of seven monuments (with numbers) located in Washington, D.C.: 1. The Vietnam Veterans Memorial, 2. Arlington National Cemetery, 3. The Jefferson Memorial, 4. The Lincoln Memorial, 5. The Marine Corps War Memorial, 6. The Roosevelt Memorial, and 7. The Washington Monument. Have them speculate about the purpose of each monument. Explain to the students that they will have an opportunity to research each monument and discover where it is located on the map of the D.C. area.

Teaching the Lesson:

1. Divide the class into seven groups, one to research each monument. Assign the groups a monument to research by randomly distributing the cards to the groups.
2. Distribute a copy of page 18 to each group. Allow the groups to access the Internet, gather their information, and mark the location of their monument by writing the number on the Mall map. (The Marine Corps War Memorial is located near Arlington National Cemetery, and the Roosevelt Memorial is in West Potomac Park on the Tidal Basin.)
3. Students each transfer their sketches from the research guide onto a three-by-five-inch note card and cut it out around its outline. They secure it next to the location they marked on the map by folding the bottom edge of the picture back and gluing the tab to the poster board. Then they summarize the information they learned on an additional note card, including the name of the monument and the number. (Each monument on the map has a number next to it and a corresponding number on the card that gives details about it.)
4. Secure all the cards to one sheet of construction paper.
5. Display the completed three-dimensional Washington, D.C., map and cards in the library or on a table in the front office.

Activities:

- Students may elect to create a simple three-dimensional model of their monument instead of simply using a paper drawing. Supply the students with the materials they need to complete this task. Follow the steps above to complete the map.

- Have the students reflect on their knowledge of American history to design and create a model of an original monument. They make a sketch or three-dimensional image of the monument and write a summary of its purpose, following the research guide on page 18. Students share their original monument with the class.

Washington, D.C. *(cont.)*

Using your favorite search engine, run a search using the key words "Monument of Washington D.C." or the name of a specific monument. Once you have located an appropriate Web site, complete the information on this page

Directions: Click on the monuments link. Select the name of the monument you will research. Complete the information below. Use additional paper if necessary.

Name of monument _____

Number on the card _____ Year it was erected or dedicated _____

Purpose of the monument _____

_____

_____

_____

A little bit of history _____

_____

_____

Washington, D.C. *(cont.)*

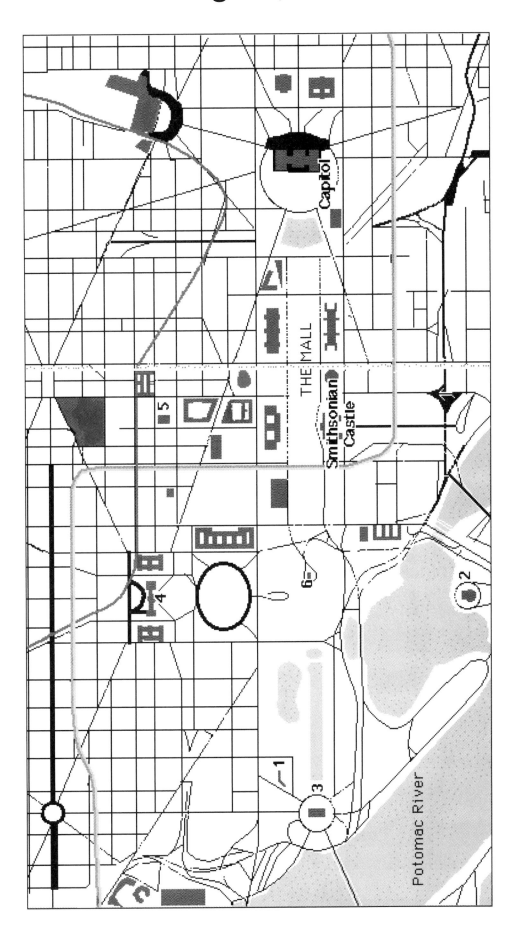

My Book of Washington, D.C.

This book will give you information about Washington, D.C. Color the pages, then cut them out on the dotted lines. Staple them together on the left-hand side to create your book.

My Book of Washington, D.C.

Name _____

Washington, D.C., is the capital of the United States of America. It is between the states of Maryland and Virginia, but it is not a state. The land is called the District of Columbia (D.C.). Find Washington, D.C., on this map.

My Book of Washington, D.C. *(cont.)*

Washington, D.C., was named in honor of George Washington, the first president of the United States. He chose the location for Washington, D.C. It is across the Potomac River from his home, Mount Vernon.

Most of the government offices for the United States are in Washington, D.C. Members of Congress make the laws for the United States. They work in the Capitol Building. This is the Capitol.

My Book of Washington, D.C. *(cont.)*

This is the White House. Construction on it began in 1792. All of the presidents except George Washington have lived here. The president's office, called the Oval Office, is in the White House, too.

This is the Washington Monument. It was built in honor of George Washington. It has flags all the way around it. You can ride to the top in an elevator. Sometimes you might walk down its 896 steps.

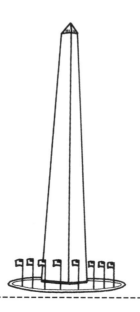

My Book of Washington, D.C. *(cont.)*

This is the Lincoln Memorial. It was built in honor of Abraham Lincoln. A huge statue of Abraham Lincoln sitting in a chair is inside the memorial.

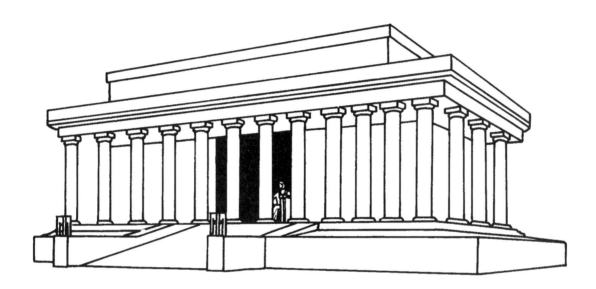

The Smithsonian Institution is the world's largest group of museums and art galleries. Most of its buildings are in Washington, D.C.

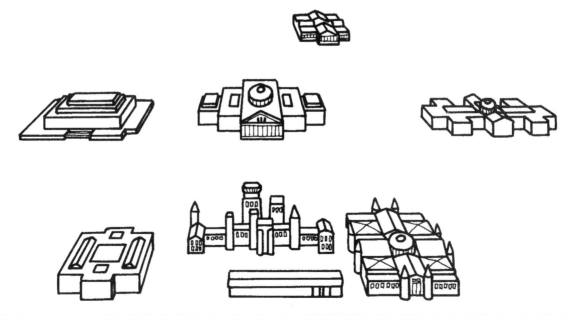

23

Underground Railroad

Harriet Tubman

The Underground Railroad wasn't really a railroad. It was a network of people who helped African-American slaves in the Southern United States escape to freedom in the free states and Canada before the Civil War. A group of Quakers started the Underground Railroad in 1780.

Most of the slaves who escaped through the Underground Railroad were young men. They would travel at night, using the North Star to guide them. These men stayed with sympathetic free African Americans at farms or houses in town, slowly making their way north.

Harriet Tubman was one of the most famous rescuers of slaves. A former slave herself, she returned to the South nineteen times during her life to help free other slaves. Levi Coffin, a Quaker from Cincinnati, was also famed for his help in rescuing slaves.

The work done by the Underground Railroad helped people in the northern United States understand the horrors of slavery.

Activity: Visit the following Web site: *http://www.incwell.com/Biographies/Tubman.html*. Below, write down three interesting facts that you learned about Harriet Tubman.

_____

_____

_____

_____

_____

_____

The Jane Addams Hull House Museum

Hull House was a settlement house—a charitable establishment set up to provide help for poor people. These houses were established in the late 19th and early 20th centuries. The Jane Addams Hull House Museum is a monument which honors Jane Addams, her work, and the Chicago neighborhood she fought to improve.

Hull House was founded in 1889 by Jane Addams (1860–1935) and her friend Ellen Gates Starr. Needy families came here for food and other forms of help. Children living in poverty could come here to participate in recreational activities. Hull House also served immigrants who had just arrived in the United States. Here, they received assistance with English and American citizenship.

Jane Addams was a social reformer who won the Nobel Peace Prize for her work with poor Americans. She fought for immigrants' rights, education for all children, and labor reform. Later, she wrote a book called *Twenty Years at Hull House.*

Hull House was originally located in a single building called the Hull Mansion. Later, it grew to 13 buildings that housed meeting rooms, a gymnasium, a day nursery, a recreation room, arts and crafts rooms, adult classrooms, a music school, a theater, and a social center. Private citizens contributed money to keep Hull House in operation.

Hull House was restored by the University of Illinois at Chicago in the mid-1960s. Today, the Jane Addams Hull House Museum is housed in two of the original 13 buildings. Visitors will find furniture, paintings, and photographs of Jane Addams, Ellen Gates Starr, and the people they served.

Activity: Visit the following Web site: *http://www.uic.edu/jaddams/hull/wajayr.html* and print out the information on books about Jane Addams. Take the list to your local or school library and check out a book on Addams' life. On a separate sheet of paper write a paragraph about what you learned from this book.

The Statue of Liberty

The Statue of Liberty stands as a memorial to international freedom. It was created to celebrate the friendship between France and the United States during the American Revolution (1775–1783). The Statue was designed by French sculptor Frédéric-Auguste Bartholdi. The iron frame was created by French engineer Gustave Alexandre, the same man who built the Eiffel Tower in Paris. The French people donated the money for the statue which was first exhibited in Paris before being shipped to America.

The statue of Liberty is located on Liberty Island in New York City. It was dedicated by United States President Grover Cleveland on October 28, 1886, and proclaimed a national monument in 1924. The statue was often the first thing that thousands of visitors and immigrants saw as they approached America by ship for the first time.

The statue's formal name is Liberty Enlightening the World. It shows a woman escaping from chains, which lie at her feet. The chains symbolize persecution. Her right hand holds a burning torch that represents liberty. Her left hand holds a tablet inscribed with the date "July 4, 1776," the day the United States declared its independence from Britain. The seven rays of her spiked crown symbolize the seven seas and continents.

The Statue of Liberty is 151 feet (46 m) high. The base and pedestal increase its height to 305 feet (93 m). Ferries from Battery Park in New York City take visitors to Liberty Island. Visitors can climb 192 steps to an observation area and museum at the top of the pedestal. The full climb of 354 steps takes visitors from the pedestal to Liberty's crown. Here they can look out over New York Harbor and the city.

The Statue of Liberty Activities

- An inscription is on the pedestal for all to read and consider. Invite the students to do the same. This inscription is a poetic account of Lady Liberty's thoughts, written by Emma Lazarus, as she welcomes newcomers to America. Visit this Web site to view the whole poem: *http://www.teachercreated.com/books/2403.* Click on page 44, site 1.

- Read the entire inscription once. Ask the students what they think the message as a whole is trying to relay. Then break the poem up into sections. Have student teams further reflect on the meaning of the section assigned to them. Then come together as a class to discuss the whole poem again.

- Lead a discussion about liberty and freedom. What do these terms mean to the students? The Statue of Liberty is but one of many symbols to signify both the liberty and freedom we as Americans value and immigrants to our nation seek. Have the students list other symbols to represent these concepts (*Uncle Sam, bald eagle, presidential seal, the flag, the Liberty Bell, etc.*). Discuss some liberties and freedoms we sometimes take for granted. Then have the students write a short essay entitled "What Freedom Means to Me." Post the essays on a bulletin board with an enlargement of the Statue of Liberty.

- Have the students use clay to mold a replica of the Statue of Liberty. They may use toothpicks or craft sticks to etch the finer details. Mount the statues on pieces of blue construction paper or poster board (to act as New York Harbor). Select two or three students to write facts about her on note cards. Then put the students' creations on display in the media center with the fact cards. Visitors will not be able to resist a peek at the models, and they will learn interesting information, too.

Monument Picture Match

Using the words in the word box, label the monuments.

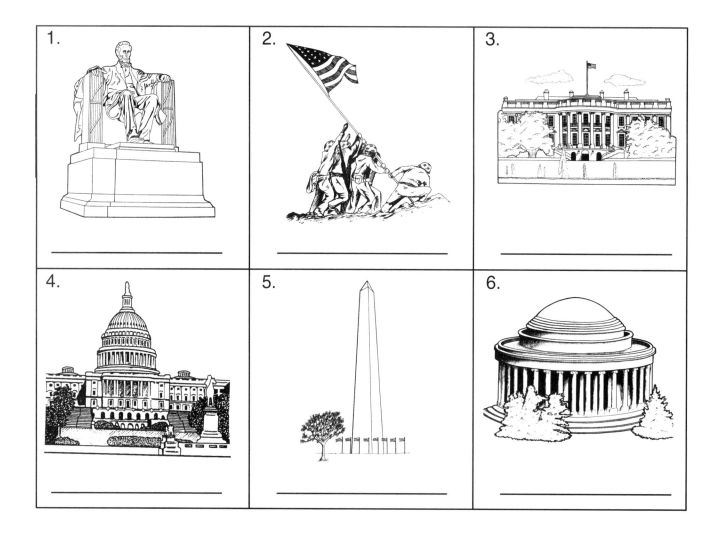

1. _____

2. _____

3. _____

4. _____

5. _____

6. _____

Word Box

Jefferson Memorial	White House	Capitol
Washington Monument	Lincoln Memorial	Marine Corps War Memorial

Note to teacher: You may cut apart the pictures and name labels, glue them to index cards, and use them as a concentration-style matching game.

Mount Rushmore

Mount Rushmore is a national memorial located in the Black Hills of South Dakota. It features the heads of George Washington, Thomas Jefferson, Abraham Lincoln, and Theodore Roosevelt carved out of the granite rim of Mount Rushmore. The sculpture stands 500 feet (152 m) above the valley floor. It cost almost a million dollars to create.

Historian Doane Robertson first came up with the idea for the sculpture in the 1920s. Gutzon Borglum designed the memorial to serve as a tribute to the growth of the United States and the importance of its leaders. He began construction on the memorial in 1927. Workers used drills and dynamite to carve out each head. Borglum died before the last head—that of Theodore Roosevelt—was completed in 1941. His son, Lincoln, completed work on the sculpture.

Visitors to Mount Rushmore can see Gutzon Borglum's studio, located near the monument. Inside, they can look at the plaster casts and tools he used to create this sculpture.

Activity: Which four presidents would you have included on Mount Rushmore? Why would you have chosen them? In the space below, answer these questions in paragraph form.

_____

_____

_____

_____

_____

_____

_____

_____

_____

_____

Crazy Horse Memorial

The Crazy Horse Memorial is currently being built to honor Native Americans in North America. Crazy Horse (1843–1877) was a much-respected Sioux chief who fought to keep Native American land in the Black Hills of South Dakota.

Korczak Ziolkowski (1908–1982) was a sculptor who assisted Gutzon Borglum with the creation of Mount Rushmore. In 1939, the Lakota Native American tribe asked him to sculpt Crazy Horse into the 600-foot Thunderhead Mountain, which is part of the Black Hills. The memorial was dedicated on June 3, 1948. Five of the nine survivors of the Battle of Little Bighorn attended the dedication. When it is completed, the sculpture will depict the famous chief riding astride a horse.

Korczak Ziolokowsi also designed The Indian Museum of North America. The museum currently houses thousands of artifacts belonging to the Native Americans of North America. Eventually, the museum will relocate to the base of the mountain. It will be created out of pieces of rock blasted from the mountain in the process of sculpting Crazy Horse.

Although Korcazk Ziolkowski died in 1982, his family dedicated themselves to seeing his dream of the completed monument come true. They have been organizing work on the memorial for the last two decades.

Activity: On the map of South Dakota, locate the Black Hills, the Crazy Horse Memorial, and Mount Rushmore.

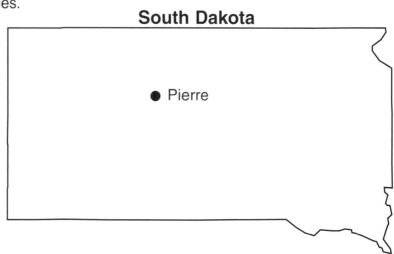

South Dakota

● Pierre

The Trail of Tears

The Trail of Tears refers to the route that Native Americans walked from their homes in Georgia to Oklahoma. In 1830, the United States Congress passed the Indian Removal Act, which was signed into law by President Andrew Jackson. The Cherokee tribe tried to fight this law by creating an independent Cherokee Nation.

In spite of this new nation, the United States began to enforce Native American relocation to Oklahoma in 1938. Men, women, and children were forced to march 1,000 miles across the country. Over 4,000 Native Americans died during this journey. This is why they called it The Trail of Tears.

The American statesman Henry Clay called President Jackson's enforcement of the Native American removal a stain on the nation's honor. These days, most people regard the forced taking of Native American land as a tragedy. We can follow the route that the Native Americans took from Georgia to Oklahoma, in our cars, on busses, on bicycles, or on foot.

Activity: Study the map below. Then, on a separate sheet of paper, write a journal entry describing how you would feel if you were one of the Native Americans forced to leave your home.

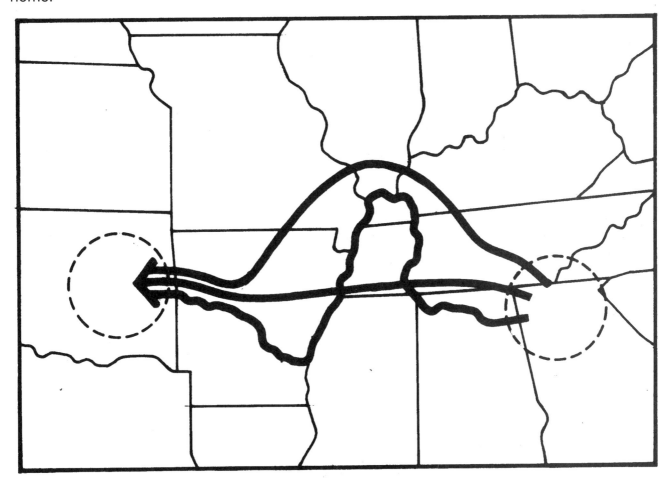

The Supreme Court

The Supreme Court is the highest court in the national judiciary. Its main duty is to interpret the Constitution of the United States in order to uphold the law. The Court's main offices are located in Washington, D.C. Although the Supreme Court held its first session on February 2, 1790, it did not have its own building until 1935, 145 years later.

Chief Justice William Howard Taft, who had served as president of the United States from 1909 to 1913, decided that the Supreme Court needed a permanent home. The Supreme Court building was designed by architect Cass Gilbert. It is located in Washington, D.C. The building is made of marble. It is four stories tall. There are marble figures seated on either side of the building's main steps. On the left side is a female figure titled The Contemplation of Justice. A male figure titled the Guardian or Authority of Law sits on the right side.

The Supreme Court is in session from October until May or June each year. It consists of eight associate justices and the chief justice. All justices are elected for life. Thurgood Marshall became the first African-American justice in 1967. Judge Sandra Day O'Connor became the first female justice in 1981.

Activity: Use an encyclopedia, a search engine, or other reference to research one of the cases brought to the Supreme Court. Then answer the questions below.

1. What is the name of the case you researched?

    _____

    _____

2. What was the problem that inspired this case?

    _____

    _____

3. What was the outcome of this case?

    _____

    _____

4. How have Americans been affected by the outcome of this case?

    _____

    _____

The United Nations

The United Nations Headquarters of the World Organization is located in New York City. It is an international zone that belongs to all member states. It has its own security force, fire department, and postal administration. In fact, it even has its own stamps! These stamps can only be mailed from United Nations Headquarters, so visitors love to send postcards to friends and relatives from these buildings.

The United Nations is an international organization created to promote peace between countries. It was established after World War Two ended in 1945.

The Headquarters consists of four main buildings that were designed by an international team of architects and completed in 1952. Along First Avenue, visitors can see the colorful display of flags belonging to the different countries that are members of the United Nations. The flags have been placed in alphabetical order. The garden outside the United Nations Headquarters contains sculptures donated from many different countries. Inside the buildings, visitors can see a stained glass window donated by French artist Marc Chagall, a Japanese peace bell, and a Chinese ivory carving.

Activity: The United Nations has its own stamps. On a separate piece of paper design a stamp that would be representative of the United Nations.

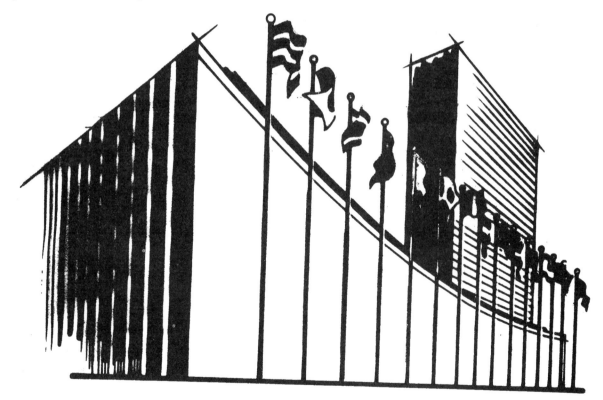

Internet Activity

For more information on the United Nations, go to the link below. You can see the flags belonging to the different member nations, learn about special days and anniversaries, look at art made by students all over the world, and explore facts about various countries.

http://www.un.org/Pubs/CyberSchoolBus/index.html

Martin Luther King, Jr., National Historic Site

The Martin Luther King, Jr., National Historic Site includes his birth home, church, and grave site in Atlanta, Georgia. Martin Luther King, Jr., (1929–1968) was a man who dedicated his life to civil rights. He was awarded the Nobel Peace Prize for his work to ensure equal rights for African Americans during the 1950s and 1960s. He was assassinated in 1968.

Martin Luther King, Jr., was born in a frame house on Auburn Avenue. He attended Ebenezer Baptist Church, just a few blocks away. Both King and his father preached at this church.

The historic districts included in the Martin Luther King, Jr., National Historic Site were home to many African Americans in the late 1800s and early 1900s. After the Civil War, African Americans built businesses, houses, and churches on these streets. Many of these buildings are still standing.

Next to the church that King both attended and preached at, visitors will find a memorial park. This is the location of Martin Luther King, Jr.'s crypt.

The Martin Luther King, Jr., Center for Nonviolent Social Change, Inc. stands across from the church. People at this Center work to continue King's goal of social equality and peace. The Visitor's Center at this monument features exhibits about Martin Luther King, Jr., as well as information on the Civil Rights movement.

Activity: Martin Luther King, Jr., is famous for his "I Have a Dream" speech. Find a copy of the speech to either read or listen to. Afterwards, write what your dreams for the world might be.

United States Holocaust Memorial Museum

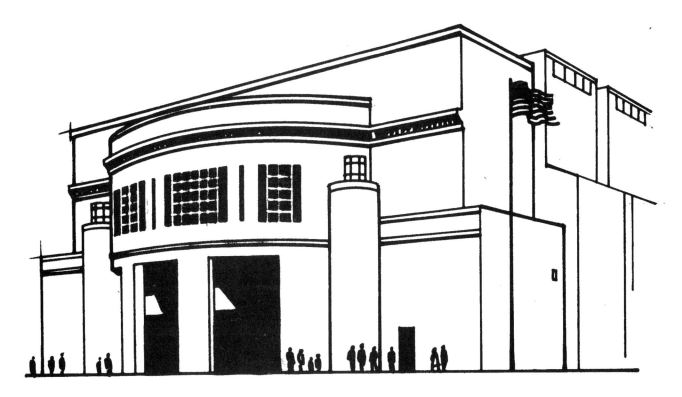

Congress authorized the United States Holocaust Memorial Museum in 1980. The memorial is dedicated to preserving the history of the persecution and murder of over six million Jewish people and millions of other victims who were killed during the Holocaust by the Nazis between 1933 and 1945.

The Holocaust Memorial Museum officially opened in Washington, D.C., in 1993. James I. Freed designed the building. As a child, Freed escaped the Nazis by fleeing with his family from Germany to the United States. The museum he designed reflects some of the architecture used in Nazi concentration camps.

The main feature in this museum is the permanent exhibition, which tells the story of the Holocaust through photographs, films, artifacts, and oral histories. Sometimes people who survived the Holocaust come to the museum and speak with visitors. The Hall of Remembrance is located at the end of the museum's permanent exhibition. It is the official national monument to those who were killed in the Holocaust.

There are two special exhibitions designed for children. One is titled Daniel's Story: Remember the Children. The other is the Children's Wall, dedicated to the children who died during the Holocaust.

Activity: What type of tribute would you design dedicated to young children who died during the Holocaust? Write or draw your tribute.

Monuments and Statues

1. What does the statue on top of the Capitol Building represent?

   _____

2. What famous statue is located in New York City's harbor?

   _____

3. What famous memorial in Washington, D.C., is surrounded by hundreds of Japanese cherry trees?

   _____

4. Three monuments in Washington, D.C., were erected in honor of what men?

   _____

5. Where is the Tomb of the Unknown Soldier?

   _____

6. Where is the Marine Corps War Memorial located?

   _____

7. A monument in Atlanta, Georgia, memorializes what man?

   _____

8. What monument was erected in Washington, D.C., in honor of the people who died during the war in Vietnam?

   _____

9. A monument in Chicago, Illinois, memorializes what woman?

   _____

10. The White House has been the residence for all but which U.S. president?

   _____

Design Your Own Monument or Memorial

If you could construct a monument or memorial such as those you have studied in this book, what would you create? To what/whom would your monument or memorial be dedicated?

Materials: construction paper, pencils, glue, toothpicks, pipe cleaners, plastic tape, old clothes, wire hangers, newspaper, sand, clay, paint, and any other materials that one might use to create a monument—the more creative the materials, the better!

Directions: Design and build your miniature monument, and then answer the questions below.

1. What is the name of your monument?

   _____

2. What or whom does your monument memorialize?

   _____

Draw a picture of your monument in the space below.

National Parks

The United States has many national parks that are protected by the government. The government makes sure that people don't build, hunt, log, or mine in these parks so that people may observe the land in its natural state.

In 1864, President Abraham Lincoln signed an agreement preserving the Yosemite Valley in California for public recreation. Yellowstone National Park became the first official national park in 1872, when President Ulysses S. Grant signed the Yellowstone Act. During the 1890s, three more areas of wilderness became national parks. These include Yosemite, Sequoia, and Mt. Rainier National Parks.

In 1916, Congress established a National Park Service. This is a branch of the Department of the Interior. It is responsible for taking care of these wilderness areas. National parks may be threatened by a variety of problems. Some of these include fires, too much traffic, people who trample delicate plants and poach animals and birds, erosion, and lack of money for upkeep of these important lands.

National preserves are often located in or near national parks. These preserves are set aside for wildlife preservation and study instead of human recreation. Scientists can observe plant and animal life in their natural habitat at national preserves. The United States set aside its first natural preserves in 1974. In the 1980s, many new national parks and preserves were created in America.

Sometimes national parks are set up to preserve the history of a country. The United States is home to the Klondike Gold Rush National History Park in Alaska. Prospectors traveled on this land to the Yukon Territory during the stampede of 1897–98. The Gettysburg National Military Park in Pennsylvania marks the site of an important battle in the Civil War (1861–1865).

National parks and preserves have been set aside for the enjoyment of people, as well as for the preservation of animals and plants. Visitors to these parks should stay on marked trails and refrain from picking plants and feeding wild animals. In this way, we can all help to preserve wilderness in the United States.

Activity: What are ways you can help to preserve the environment? On the back of this page list as many ideas as you can think of and discuss them with your classmates.

Research National Parks and Preserves

There are many national parks and preserves in the United States. Using the Internet or an encyclopedia, choose one national park or preserve and write a report about it in the space below.

Make sure to answer the five journalistic questions in your report:
Who? **What?** **Why?** **When?** **Where?** **How?**

_____
Name of National Park or Preserve

_____

_____

_____

_____

_____

_____

_____

_____

_____

_____

_____

_____

_____

_____

_____

Grand Canyon National Park

Grand Canyon National Park was officially established by United States Congress in 1919. It is located in Northern Arizona. The canyon was carved by the Colorado River. It is 277 miles (446 km) long. It is 18 miles (20 km) wide and is more than 5,000 feet (1,500 m) deep. It includes both the Grand Canyon National Monument and the Marble Canyon National Monument. The Canyon is bordered on the south by the Havasupai Native-American Reservation.

Prehistoric Native-American groups lived in the Grand Canyon and on its rim. Visitors to the canyon can still see cliff dwellings built by the Anasazi and the ruins of Native-American pueblos. In 1869, the explorer John Wesley Powell and ten friends traveled through the canyon in four rowboats. This marked the first passage down the canyon by a European explorer.

The Grand Canyon is home to deer, cougar, antelope, and mountain sheep. Visitors will see trees including aspen, fir, pine, spruce, pinon, and juniper. One of the rock formations is known as "The Alligator" because that is what it looks like! Due to the light, the rock layers found in the Grand Canyon look like they change during the day, so the canyon you're looking at in the morning may look much different in the evening.

Activity: Describe what you think a trip through the Grand Canyon would be like. If you have taken this trip, include some of the experiences you had while there.

Petroglyph National Monument

Petroglyph National Monument was established in 1990 by the National Park Service. It is located in Albuquerque, New Mexico. The monument stretches 7,100 acres and features a collection of Indian and Hispanic rock art. The monument also contains over 100 archaeological sites and protected wildlife habitats.

Petroglyphs are symbols carved into stones. Some symbols include animal shapes, stars, spirals, geometric shapes, and masks that tell about society and religion. The Pueblo people from this area used petroglyphs to communicate with each other. Most of the petroglyphs were created between the years 1300 and 1650, though some could be between 2,000 and 3,000 years old!

You can see photographs of Petroglyph National Monument at the Web site below:

http://istvan.com/petroglyphs/gallery.html

Activity: What symbols would you use to communicate with another person if you couldn't speak or write a common language? Together with a partner, create a list of ten symbols. Draw them in the space below, and then explain what each symbol stands for.

Symbol	What it stands for	Symbol	What it stands for
1.		6.	
2.		7.	
3.		8.	
4.		9.	
5.		10.	

Build an Edible Memorial

Using common foods, students can build their own edible monuments.

Materials: graham crackers or other types of crackers (It's fun to have a variety of shapes and sizes on hand.), marshmallow cream or peanut or almond butter, plastic knives, paper cups, spoons, paper, pencil, paper towels

Directions: Give every student a piece of paper and a pencil. Ask them to each sketch a design for their monument. While they are drawing, put out a variety of different-sized crackers and peanut or almond butter. (To keep this project very simple, use graham crackers and marshmallow cream.)

After students have completed their drawings, ask them to take a paper towel, plastic knife, and some crackers. You can spoon peanut or almond butter or marshmallow cream into paper cups for students to use as "mortar." Explain to students that they will be building their monument out of crackers. Walk around and assist students as needed.

When students have completed their buildings, go around the room and ask each student to hold up his/her sketch. Compare the drawing to the edible monument. Then invite students to eat their monuments as a snack. **Note:** Check for any food allergies before allowing students to eat their creations.

You might choose to take photographs of students with their completed monuments before they eat them.

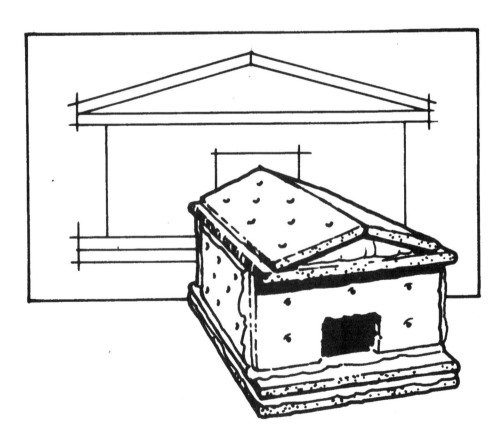

Monument Riddles

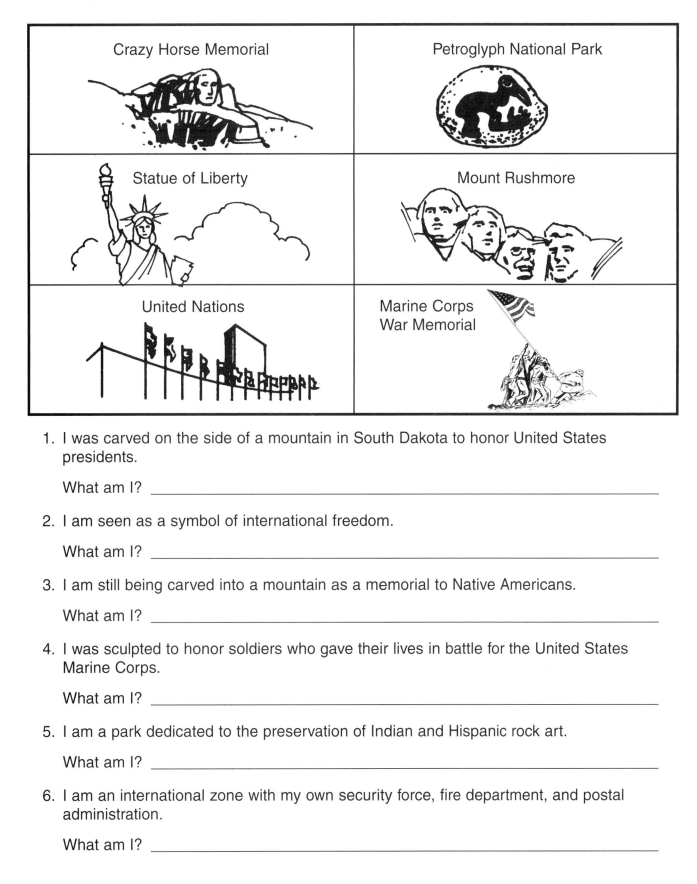

Crazy Horse Memorial	Petroglyph National Park
Statue of Liberty	Mount Rushmore
United Nations	Marine Corps War Memorial

1. I was carved on the side of a mountain in South Dakota to honor United States presidents.

   What am I? _____

2. I am seen as a symbol of international freedom.

   What am I? _____

3. I am still being carved into a mountain as a memorial to Native Americans.

   What am I? _____

4. I was sculpted to honor soldiers who gave their lives in battle for the United States Marine Corps.

   What am I? _____

5. I am a park dedicated to the preservation of Indian and Hispanic rock art.

   What am I? _____

6. I am an international zone with my own security force, fire department, and postal administration.

   What am I? _____

National Landmarks and Memorials

Using the Internet or an encyclopedia, find the location of the American landmarks and memorials.

1. Crazy Horse _____

2. Grand Canyon _____

3. Petroglyph National Park _____

4. Trail of Tears _____

5. Klondike Gold Rush National History Park _____

6. Gettysburg Military National Park_____

7. The Alamo _____

8. Yellowstone National Park _____

9. The Painted Desert _____

10. The Grand Canyon_____

11. The Bad Lands_____

12. Niagara Falls _____

13 Old Faithful _____

14. Death Valley _____

15. Mount McKinley _____

16. Glacier National Park _____

Research a Monument

There are many other monuments in the United States that have not been mentioned in this book. Using the Internet, as well as encyclopedias and books, research another monument and write a short report about it in the space below. Illustrate your report.

Make sure to answer the five journalistic questions in your report:

Who?   **What?**   **Why?**   **When?**   **Where?**   **How?**

_____

Name of Monument

_____

_____

_____

_____

_____

_____

_____

_____

_____

_____

_____

Monumental Recipes

Some storytellers say that when George Washington was a little boy, his father gave him a hatchet. Young George tried to cut down a cherry tree with his new toy. When his father asked him about the marks in the tree, George supposedly replied, "I cannot tell a lie. I did it with my hatchet." Whether or not the story is true, George Washington has always been associated with honesty and cherries. To celebrate his birthday on February 21, you may choose to make the following recipe with your students.

Cherry S'mores

Ingredients:
1 cup (236 ml) marshmallow cream
1 cup (236 ml) dried tart cherries
1/2 cup (118 ml) semisweet chocolate chips
24 graham cracker squares

Directions: Put marshmallow cream, cherries, and chocolate chips in a medium bowl and mix well. Place six of the graham crackers on a microwave-safe plate. Spoon a heaping tablespoon of marshmallow mixture on each cracker. Top with remaining crackers. Microwave, uncovered, on high 30 to 45 seconds, or until marshmallow mixture is soft and warm. Carefully remove plate from the microwave and set on a hot pad. Let s'mores cool slightly before eating them. (Makes 12 s'mores.)

Frybread was a main staple made by southwestern Native-American women on early reservations in the United States. Using government rations, they made this bread and stuffed it with meat for tacos or with berry pudding for dessert. Each cook formed her bread into a particular shape; the shape of the bread affected how it cooks. Let your students experiment with different shapes and thicknesses of bread dough.

Frybread

Ingredients:
2 cups (473.2 ml) flour
1 tablespoon (14.8 ml) baking powder
1 teaspoon (4.9 ml) salt
1 cup (236 ml) milk
Canola oil heated in frypan or electric skillet

Directions: Sift dry ingredients. Lightly stir in milk. Add more flour as necessary to make a workable dough. Knead the dough on a floured board with floured hands until smooth. Pinch off fist-sized balls and let students shape them into a disk. Fry in oil heated to about 375°F (176°C) until golden and done on both sides, about 5 minutes. **Use extreme caution when using hot oil**. Drain on absorbent paper and serve with jam or powdered sugar on top. (Makes 8–10 small rounds of bread.)

Suggestions for Teachers

- There are many other projects that students may complete to supplement their study of United States monuments and memorials.

- You may choose to watch videotapes about monuments or memorials in your class. Then discuss with students what they noticed about these places.

- Ask students to which monuments and memorials they themselves have been. If possible, arrange with parents a show-and-tell presentation. Students can bring in souvenirs, photos, maps, slides, and other evidence of their visits.

- Arrange a field trip to a local monument or memorial. Every city has such places, and some are within walking distance. Study the history of your local monument or memorial before you take your field trip. Afterwards, invite students to draw or write about the place they visited. Here are some ideas for local monuments and memorials: the first house in your area, a statue dedicated to someone in your area, the first local store or church, a garden dedicated to a local person, or even a graveyard!

- Check out books on specific monuments and memorials, and put them in your classroom reading center. Students will enjoy looking at full-color photographs of national parks and wildlife preserves, as well as pictures of the political and social monuments they've studied.

- Students can choose individual monuments or memorials on which to report. They can write to the visitors' center for information, conduct research on the Internet and in the library, and then write a report or give an oral presentation.

Answer Key

Page 4

1. 1793
2. Washington, D.C.
3. white marble
4. more than twice its original size
5. the Rotunda, the Senate Chamber, the House Chamber, the President's Room, the National Statuary Hall

Page 30

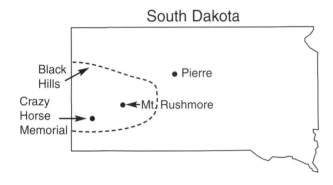

South Dakota

Black Hills

Crazy Horse Memorial

Pierre

Mt. Rushmore

Page 36

1. She represents freedom.
2. Statue of Liberty
3. the Jefferson Memorial
4. Thomas Jefferson, George Washington, Abraham Lincoln
5. Arlington National Cemetery in Virginia
6. Washington, D.C.
7. Martin Luther King, Jr.
8. Vietnam Veterans Memorial
9. Jane Addams
10. George Washington

Page 43

1. Mount Rushmore
2. Statue of Liberty
3. Crazy Horse Memorial
4. Marine Corps War Memorial
5. Petroglyph National Park
6. United Nations

Page 44

1. South Dakota
2. Arizona
3. New Mexico
4. It begins in Georgia and ends in Oklahoma.
5. Alaska
6. Pennsylvania
7. Texas
8. Wyoming (and Montana and Idaho)
9. Arizona
10. Arizona
11. South Dakota
12. New York
13. Wyoming
14. California
15. Alaska
16. Montana